Meanderings of the Heart

━ ▪ ━ ▪ ━ ▪ ━ ▪ ━

The Poetry of Dolores Kennelly

Meanderings of the Heart

— ∎ — ∎ — ∎ — ∎ —

Intrepid **Ink**

Published by Intrepid Ink Publishing

ISBN 13: 978-1-937022-85-3

Printed in the United States of America

Foreword

For Dolores Kennelly, life's road has had many turns, some snow soft dreamy, others harsh detours bringing unwanted change -- from the one room unheated school house in the farthest corner of Wisconsin, to experience seventy years of change in Milwaukee.

Written words have always recorded the smiles and sorrows or glory's and grief's of mothering eight transracial children, and the happy continuing story of many grandchildren and great grandchildren.

After the recent heart heavy loss of a precious daughter, the road still winds on ahead, a path of memories and new mornings.

Celebration

With all my heart dedicated to Kaliyah, Savannah and Nero.

Little pretty,
Tiny little person, my
Heart belongs to
You in a way no
One ever has owned
It ---- and I --- older
Now, and not as
Questioning – simply see
Jesus in your smile – and
God in your eyes and
His holy spirit singing
In your laughter
Always clapping precious
Hands – scream your own
Joy – reach for Grampa to play
Upside cuddle –up and go to
Sleep, a thousand times with
Grama --- thinking back --- the
Delivery room where Daddy and Grama
Could feel God bring you into
This world and
Time is not
Always a friend ----

Table Of Contents

A Circle?

We gather in
the bonds of
fellowship and
are encircled by
His love ...
but the
very circle that
surrounds us also
blinds our eyes
to those outside
it's warmth- and they
silently wait, tucked away
in attic rooms, and on
the shelves of
darkened flats across
our towns and cities,
with fear their
full-time
occupation- and we
selfishly do not
take that one
step apart
that would widen
our circle and
make room
for them ... what if
our circle grows
so small it
becomes
more narrow
than round?

Promise

There are storms that
I have weathered . . . others
there will be. But strength
is born while battles rage
and truth is found anew in fury.
If the climb has been uphill
against the downpour and torrent,
there has always been sunshine
at the summit, and quiet
after the thunderclap . . . and now
while these waters roll and the
winds encompass me, I will
remember the calm,
and my spirit will walk
on the waters after all . . . if I
don't forget the rainbows
there have been, and those
that yet will be.

This Much, Lord

When I hear Your lovely
voice, Lord, Jesus,
asking if I love You
more than these? . . .
let me be slow to
answer and know
whereof I speak . . .
Be sure it is the
truth I tell, not
forgetting the idols
I hold up, nor the things
I may put first . . . Be
certain that I consider
the measure of my
witness and the
surrender of myself;
and let me weigh my
love for others on
the scale of Your question
and answer as I should-
even if it hurts.

Step By Step

An ocean
is
a mighty thing,
but for all
its vastness, only
one drop at
a time, And
mountains, however
tall they
rise, are just
one grain of
God's good
earth upon
another, and life
is thus too- for all
its height and
depth we
can live it
but one short
moment at
a time; Give
us then, dear
Builder of Men,
That measure
Of grace to help
us live it
well, one minute
after
another . . . . . Amen!

Thy Rod and Thy Staff . . .

Dear Gentle Shepherd
You
Keep leading
me
even when
I
behave more like
a mule
than a lamb
of Yours
You choose the
pasture,
reach out
Your
staff
and point to
the
Living Water when
I fail to
see it
sparkle.
In my stubbornness
I struggle over
the
craggy peaks when
You
would show me the turquoise
softness
of the valleys
where
quiet is.
Help me to
remember
where it is that
a
lamb belongs . . .
WITHIN THE FOLD
Amen!

I Prayed

I prayed for the
bitterness I
saw in the
heart of the
friend I
love so
well . . . Prayed
that God would
soften him and
turn him
right around . . . I
prayed for his
peace of mind and
peace with his
fellow-men; and for
the anger he
displayed and
restlessness
within; but
God, whose mysteries
we cannot know,
answered my prayer
in His own way and
turned me
around instead!

Solace and Silence

In this
room I
knew
my children—Held
them
close and
heard
them sleep soft
breaths of innocence;
warm and
soft and
pure—Here I
heard them cry
and stir at
early
dawn, and in
this room though
time has tried to
change the
room (and
me) I feel
them yet—

The Full Heart

So much
has
been written
about
the hum of a bee
the song of a bird
the blue of the sky
the mystery of the
unfolding flower,
the wonder of a new life,
Springtime! So
many poems, flowery
verses, reverent
prayers, poetic
phrases; all the
heart-cry of people
who marveled at
Creation and
needed
to express that
wonder. However much
may have been
said or
penned, IT IS
NOT ENOUGH!

Quiet

Words... we
use
too many
of
them, Lord. One
time we
call it
communication, and
another time
we say it
is just a
rambling expression
of our
cluttered
minds. Give us
more time
for that
silence in
the midst of
chaos, to
hear the
THUNDERINGS and
the whispers
of Your still,
small voice.

For Everything—A Time

The story
is told
of the little
boy
who went into
his
mother's garden
opening
delicate rose
buds with his
hands.
"I'm helping,
God,"
he said.
I wonder
how
often I
have
forgotten
to
leave the
timing
in His almighty
hands,
and thus
destroyed the
promise of the
flower, and
never
really knew
what
might have
been.

His Garment

How beautiful
it is
to
read of those
who
but touched the
hem of Your
garment . . . and
how they were made
whole. The
years have all
brought
the telling of
other miracles; of
great and wondrous things
You have
done for
those
You love; but
there is
nothing written
or told that
stirs my
soul
so much as
kneeling; here
in the stillness
of my
room to
touch that
garment hem that
still transforms today
as then.
Praise God!

Sharing Time

I had my
coffee this
quiet afternoon
with a
dapper young
man in a
very
proper vest; and
all the
time we spent
together he
talked a
steady stream of
this and
that and other
things of
special interest to
us both. I
felt somehow, that
God is more
real to me for
that visit that we had; that
chubby little chick-a-dee and
I

A Heartful of Thanks

For November days and steady rain
Snow and sun and gathered grain
For pumpkins in a wagon
Skies dark and bright
A field full of drying wheat
Orange in a misty light—

For family and friends
And matters of the heart
for joys and sorrows—
And courage to take part-

For cold winds and warm fires,
A cat on my lap,
For feasting and foolishness
And a child taking a nap-

For good times and bad times
For good times that lie ahead
For all the gifts of life
And love not left unsaid

I CAN'T but I MIGHT!

Each one of us
ought to have
hidden away in a
secret chamber of the
heart; a special
dream of our own
that we know
might never
come true—a dream of
some peak to climb—a
translucent vision, a
story-book journey
to some other
land—some fantastic
success to be gained—or some
purple wild-flower
to be found, that
impossible goal
beyond reach but
not quite—not quite
because there is
ever in each one of
us the child-heart
that knows dreams
very often become
what is real and
whatever there is
that cannot
happen
just
might.

Together

God has for me
a race to run; yes,
a plan to follow,
a war to win and a
ministry to live out.
His job for me is mine
alone, among all the
lives of men.
My heart is overwhelmed.
To think that He, who
governs all mankind,
should have work
for me to do. I am
reminded that it is
He who makes the
assignment who must
also give the strength;
and thus I see the
magnitude of His
eternal plan—that
we should become a team!

True Value

For all that
has been
written there
are no common
people—no one
person not
special in his
own way . . . not one
plain and quiet
little man without
a place in God's
almighty plan; no
poverty stricken
widow without her
special niche in
life. . . no little
child, less pretty
than the rest, without
the right to aim for
the highest things;
it was not the
showy peacock
mentioned in His
Holy World; but
merry, busy, singing
sparrows.

Oh Lord

O, Lord, there are so
many people, and
God, I know
You love them
all—the ones with
tough veneer and
hard to reach; the
frightened, with
hurts so deep, the
guy who hides a
tear behind
dark glasses and
loud laughter; the
timid who, under
pressure know
no fear at
all. The bold
ones who
grow still
bolder in a
crowd. . they are
not just a
panorama, They
are individuals that
You love. Help me
to love them,
one
at a time, with
Your love. Mine is
so small.

Goodbyes

Dear Lord, I seem
to be
always saying
goodbyes—sending
them off to
new encounters and
experiences; while
I am
standing here
with my
my heart in
my throat; missing
them even
before they
are gone; and
hurrying into the
house to
pray for their
safety; and
I know their
going is a part
of
life's learning for
them; I suspect that
my staying at
home is a
part of mine—Lord,
give me
staying at
home and
waiting grace; It
takes a
special
kind.
Amen.

Darker Hue

You, me and he; all
Three, rushing in
different ways, all on
this same day, raindrops
dripping down our
noses and
wearing frowns
across our
faces; not
stopping even long
enough to
smile or
say hello; and
just be-
cause we do
not; all the
world wears a
darker hue

Knowledge!

O God,
When everything is
said
and done, when
that petition
has
been granted, and
my world is
sunshine
right; when all
the fun
things have
been
enjoyed, and
friendship's circle
widened; and
even selfish
desires
granted, and
there are
rainbows 'round
my shoulders
and successes in
every
endeavor, with
challenges
promising ahead;
yet is
there deep
within me
that stirring
restless feeling
and I
know, as I
never knew through
trial and
sorrow, that it
is You I
need.

Alone

Loneliness, that
aching thing
each of
us
possesses in
some
measure. Alone
in a
crowd, content
in the hush
of a
darkened
room. Stepping
across
chasms of
emptiness or
filled with
rainbow-hued
bubbles of
joy . . . it
really
all
depends on
the distance
between us
and
Jesus Christ.

New Year

New Year, I do not
fear you, standing here
at your newly opened door
for I do not stand alone.
There are other seekers
who will share your
challenge, and those
I love who will understand
when pain overwhelms.
There are the all-alone
who will need me; the
tender companion of my
heart who always prays
for me; the old friends
with whom I will pray
through your tempests,
and those new friends who
wait the unfolding of
the months.
There are the dear
neighbors who will enrich
my days, and the delightful
small people who walk in
my steps.
New Year, excitement builds
your threshold; anticipation
stretches across your
horizon; because in and
around and through every
hour there is the One who
planned it all-the Gentle
Galilean who walks beside
me and always holds my
hand.

But God

There were
storms that
raged
within me—But
God. and there were
tears
that would not
cease
following and the
heartache that
was
their cause—But
God. And there
was pain
through hours
long; unending—But
God. And there
was
sorrow in
waves that rolled
across my
soul— But   God.
Ever and
always it has
been; and
will be—
But God.

Little Boy

Such a little boy when he
first came to Sunday school; serious,
thin, somehow not like the
others. Others came too; came and
went. . . I am sorry to say we
taught them of a saviour's love, and
tried to paint for them a picture of
Calvary Ah. But God, who is God, sometimes
allows glimpses of glory. Time, our enemy has
gone unmarked; and the boy?—-grown
taller inside and out than most. Heaven
records in golden ink, the names of those he
has led to Christ

While church leaders gather
around shiny tables and
ask each other if Sunday schools are a
thing of the past?. . .no longer a tool for
evangelizing?. . .too many meetings too much
organizing that robs the quality of our
disorganized lives? Put them aside with the warm
nostalgia of Sunday night services

a man long ago knew the
answer who was called the
Nazarene. For one such little
child He would still have walked a
dusty road to bleed and
die on a
lonely cross.

All Along

9:00 A.M. on a non-typical
morning. Beds are not
made. The big house is
not picked up. Dishes gather
and stand; the usually
uncluttered table
is laden
Sunday clothes of
last eve strewn
about. . .and the
shoes-how many
pairs? Shades are
unsure whether
to be
up or down. The
usually efficient me,
still clad in
robe, hair
uncombed; make-up
stands at
Attention on a
shelf- it is morning. I
have need to
communicate this
new day with a God who
meets me as I AM
in a house AS IS,
so that I may
ask Him as He IS
to meet the
problems as THEY ARE
without any of the
sham I usually wear. Praise
His wonderful name,
This is how
He has seen me
all along

I Keep a Vigil

I keep a
vigil-where there is
silence and
sometimes uncertain
sound – where breath
grows
softer and peace is
everywhere –
where the
sunrise comes
across the early
dawn and
spreads
aqua and yellow
ribbons across the
way to home – and there on
strong wings
a lovely bird transports
her soul to
where, for today I
cannot go.

Early Morning

—in the
velvet
of
early morning
before the
light
appears I
am before my
window
watching golden
prism stars
doing
pirouettes in
the
garden of
the skies and
I am filled with
joy and
wonder that
the
Omnipotent
gardener who
planted
them
has set aside
His tools
for cultivating
the fields
of the
Universe, and
has come
during this
dawn hour
to
prayer with
me.

Sunset

I saw
the sky at
sunset and I
knew that
we
have no need to
wonder at the
beauty of Heaven, when
God creates
such
glory on an
ordinary day…and
then my
heart
remembered that
there is no
such thing
as an
ordinary day.

Blank Book

I bought a blank book to
write
these words and
wondered
why I
would need a
reason so trifling as
delicate paper and
a silver
pen unless the old,
old reason to write could
not be
found.

I wonder

writing, speaking... writing...
stories to tell — what has
been what has
not... truth or
pretend and which
is which? — the Dream or the Dreamer... the actor, the
author, the Drama of Life or
the one in the
mind?

I'm Home

"I'm home" they
call,
coming through
the
door to
shed their
hurts
and share
their news — waiting
for the familiar sound of
waiting — the
footsteps, the
tender response
that promises
the safe place, "I'm
home" — and
it is everything.

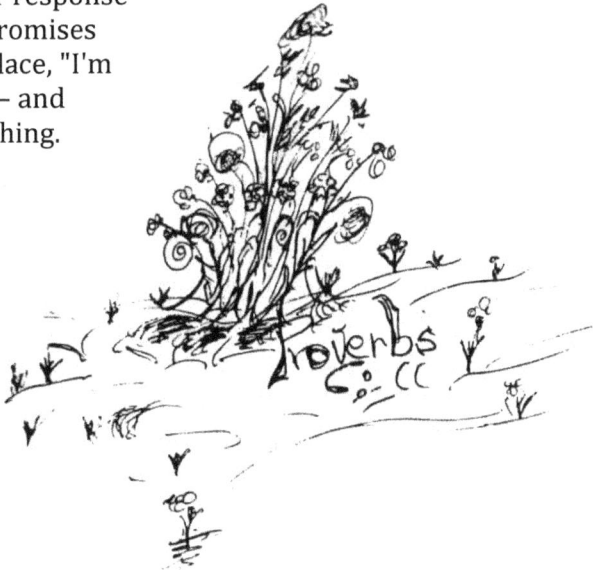

Higher

Every bright new
day is a
pilgrim journey; down
paths I
cannot
know— through the
wilderness
wanderings of
feelings that are my
own... and the
steep
steps toward
what I
know is
right.

Little Angel

Little angel, now
you're four... and I;
I can only love
you more. so
new just
four years past...
hurrying from new-
born
miraculously, moment by
memory, en-
throned in my
heart, dearer than
the
wonder of the new little
you, God's little
girl with the heavenly
face; bringing
shining here in
this special
place.

Round and Round

The wheel turns and
the water
flows —- Round and
round
and
no one
knows,
It looks so easy
and the sparkling
water sings while
the creaking
wheel grows older and
slower and
more tired
with time, round and
round and
no one knows.

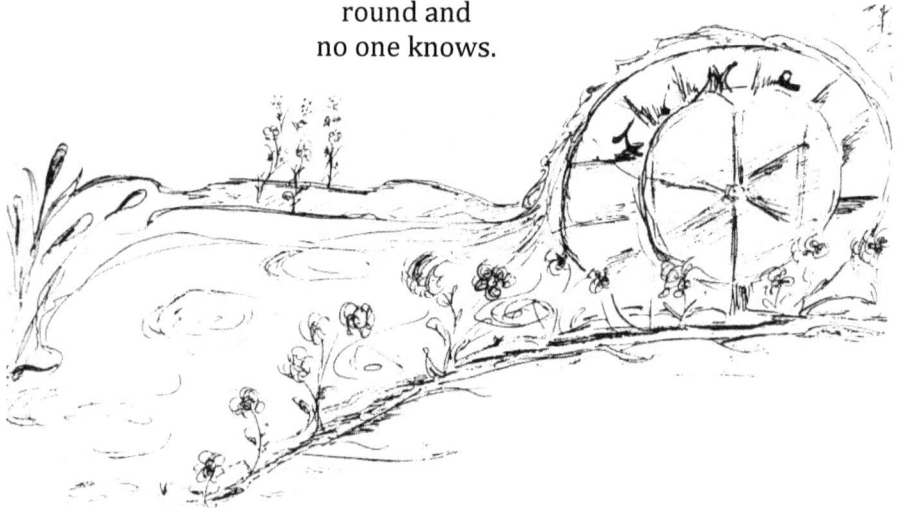

O World

O World.. world! lavender
world; I want to
hold your
morning close— it's
newness all my
own for this
one quiet hour — and the
tints cross your
sky; they are
my promise of the
pastels that will be
paralleled in my
feelings through this
day. I want to
shout... as your
golden sunrise
does — that beginning is
good and promise
is mine — I want my
song and my

responses to be
just as un-
rehearsed as your
birds I hear; and like
them too I want the
freedom to go
east or
west; and spend my
moments where my
heart is; and I want
the horizons of my
soul to stretch
far as your
pink clouds ripple; lighted
by the dawn; and
like your morning I
want it before
dusk and twilight
come.

Oh, The Glory

Oh the Glory – the Golden Glory
Of a day
In September – first
Day leaves
Fall + bring memory
Down to
Brush my
Cheek – Already wet
With a
Tear of
Joy – Yellow
Blue day
Borrowing the
Brilliance of
Last nights
Full
Moon – breathing
Nostalgia
Into still green leaves
Whispering words in
The wind -

November

PRICELESS MOMENT... I hold
you close and still and in
the blessed
silence;
sun through brown
branches and
music
box magic I am
a child
again; a child
as
old as
infinity... for I
have
learned the
rarity of YOU... PRICELESS
MOMENT

It Was God

It was God
the
gift; faithful
gift-giver who gave
your life — though
you're
much too
small to unwrap
it or
untie the
pretty ribbons of
newness — or
even
appreciate the
size of
the package that it
is — So
He has given you
from His heart, gift-keepers and
gift-carers, to
reach you Love and
warm your
world and answer your
questions — matching
your mingling tears with
their own to
teach; to smile when
your pretty balloons break.

Trains

I stand here, beside
the station, near
the tracks... watching
the trains go by; each
car filled with
laughing people on
their way to
someplace, end of the
road dreams come
true; and new
beginnings; old
places, new
spaces, and I know
that even if the
train slowed
down enough to
rush to
jump up and
....reach for the
rail, there would
be no place on
board for
those like me, who
have only grown
accustomed to the
lonely sound as
the cars roll
by.

Like Me

Lovely, Lost and
Lonely
people — Waiting
in line
to
believe — for
them
tomorrow is only
a word in
the
dictionary of
Life — on
a page they
never have
turned to and
knowing they never
will—
Like me, God
Like me?

The Learning

This almost
autumn
morning the
hours lasted too long and
cluttered
with craziness, their
hope of
meaning crashed all
around my
frustrated feelings, when a
small
brown girl stepped
up to

my heart and
the cupboard too; rolling
bumpity
cookies in her
chubby and
healing hands — — re-
minding me and re-
minding me again, of all that
matters, and all that
does not.

Disappointment

Disappoint-
ment comes
again — — no
different now than
then... Still I am
a
fool and almost be-
lieved it only to
be a
word, and had stopped be-
ing a
feeling.

This Morning

This morning
while smoky
clouds
tumble and bump against
each
other and round
silver
raindrops wiggle
in place on my
window, I
weep with them for
the friend I
need........

Fine Day

Opportunities —
changes — golden
times that
almost were — running
quickly
through all the
days
of our
Lives — wanting to
be captured, by
aching
hearts and
dreamers —
begging for the
finding — —
— — —

moving on and
out and
usually Lost —
but maybe

Requiem

...today, a tree was
felled, Just a
scrubby old maple that
I loved — — had
planted... actually... so long
ago on a day in
spring. Sadness crashed all
around me when it's
arching branches lay

cut off from
the source of their ready to
burst buds. "A life
lost" I said, "Don't be
dramatic... too sentimental"
they
said; ask if the
certain lightening would
make
it fall... but the tree, whose
life
was linked branch to
branch with
mine knew
better.

Little House

"little house"... dear
LITTLE HOUSE, you
are bigger than all
the mansions around you, and
grander, far, for you
clutch tightly the
land and the
love, the memories and the
moments... the symphony of the
seasons and the
poetry of the past, which
is, after all, "little house" the only
future we can know... so grow, grow,
grow, wild flowers and
stand, stand, stand,
"little house" for those of us who
look ahead by
holding on.

The Search

Each one of
us ought to have
hidden away in
a secret chamber of the
heart; a special
dream of our own
that we
know
might never come
true... a dream of
some peak to
climb... a
translucent vision, a
story-book
journey to some
other land' some
fantastic success to
be gained — or some
purple wildflower to
be found.
That impossible goal
beyond reach but
not quite — not
quite because there
is ever in
each one of us the
child-heart that
knows dreams very
often become what
is real and whatever there
is that cannot
happen
just might.

Temporary Tomb

The poor old
man looked through
weakened eyes at
the new
prison room that
would be home until ?
Until when? Coming
into life takes a
while, bug going out
was dragging like
his unsure
feet; and this
nursing home room
only a
temporary tomb, with
borrowed
furniture, until all the
dragging had been
done, and the room
belonged to the next on
the list.

In Between

Of humble
beginnings and
a
humbler ending but
o' the glory in be-
tween—; the honor
of hurt and the
hope of
healing... when God is
all, because all
else is
nothing.

Goodbye

sometimes LOVE is
goodbye, more often is
hello, and How are
you (really?) and Have a
good day, and Please do
well and Be careful and
See you later' but then once in a
lifetime on a
windy and
rain-swept day, it is
GOODBYE
but it is
still love.

Hurting

So many of the
shiny things so
fragile in
our hands are only
ours for such a
little while
and we are losers after
all. Those
shiny and silver and
sacred things
that happen by
the way; things that
can make a
heart remember and
maybe even
almost
forget — And
that thing which
lets light into
the darkness of an
empty soul may
be ours for
only long
enough to
touch a heart and
make it tremble
before it
breaks.

Certainty

Gentle Jesus; You
have been called the
Man of Sorrows and
You have come to
me in mine; to
know the
depths to
which despair has
driven my
spirit and it
is in that dark place You
have come with
Your compassion and
soft voice and
gentle Hands to
minister to
me and remind me
that I am
Your own; and
like dew-drops
on petals that nod
my heart is
quietly assured
that ALL I feel is
in that place
where You have
been long be-
fore me.

Toni Lee

Remember the
strawberry
party we always
meant to
have? before the
days slipped
away that were
ours then; and all
those things
we shared — done
together in
the crowd— the
pink mornings of
spring and the
secret of
the winter — but
didn't we
understand the
strawberry
seasons and the
sweet wine
of the Taste of
Life — ?

Red Wine of Life

What if I had
never known
despair and
because of it
never learned
how high I
could
fly — and if
my heart had
never ached it
might not have learned to
sing — and if sadness had
never consumed my
soul it might
never have
been
overwhelmed by
joy — and if
hatred and
anger had not
threatened my
way I would never
have known that
love could
wash it
all away and
if I had not
lived so long with
the emptiness of
not knowing
you I might never
have tasted the
fullness of the
red wine of
life...

Standing on Holy Ground

The building
was
ugly, and the
brick underneath
was paint on
top of
peeling — but the
trusting
vines hung on
and thrust their new
shoots out in
faith to grasp and grip
and grow, and
did not care if the
four ugly walls
had a
reputation — just
grew and
reached and served
it's best for
hanging on — So it
is with people I have
known
Amen —.

Dear God

Dear God, I may
as well tell
You, on this golden
glory day, that
I am afraid of
what I am
afraid of; knowing
You have
known it all
along; but You see
God, there is
none here in the
corner of
my world that I would
dare to risk
telling it
to; and so at
least if I
cannot tell him or
her or
them; I thank
You that my fears are
a part of
Your loving
me.

Wave of Sorrow

I feel a great
wave of
sorrow for
those who have
grown old; some of
them so very
old; and been
here so many
years; and yet;
have never
lived at
all; and I have
a terrible
fear inside that
circumstances and
people and
things I
cannot change
will build a
wall around
my world
and the days
that are
mine will be
numbered be-
fore the
living has really
begun —

Aching

On our rushing here and
there day we pass
almost- friends wearing
almost-smiles on their
almost-happy faces; and we
almost speak; but
we're so al-most
shy, and they all look
so al-most
cold, and we are, of
course al-most
important. And
on and on we go
until the day and the
week, and life, is
al-most over and we
keep
filling our al-most
empty hearts
with al-most full
nothings, and unless
it is on a
sad and
lonely day we
al-most never
know...

Woman

The people; those
familiar people; they
made a circle
around my
life; and they
blocked my view of
the sunshine
and their noise
shut out the
song of the
birds; and they
held their
arms (and their
needs) up high so
I could not
fly; and locked
their arms (and
their demands) so
I could not
walk away; and
they nodded their
foolish heads
and said I
was doing a
very good job; and
they never knew
that because I
could not see the
sunshine that I
loved; a part
of me had
died...

Beware

Beware, friend,
of
taking for
granted the gifts
you
mistakenly feel are
your
own — the eyes
that see; the
heart
that could but
may
not — the
little life
you help to
mold for
hope or
hopelessness, the
loved ones
you do not
know
how to
love.

Of Cliffs and Craggy Places

When I begin to
back away
from
confrontation, Lord
and only want to
dip my oars in
waters that
are stilled; re-mind me; O
please
remind me, of
what it is
that really happens to a
pool of water that
is not stirred
and then send the
bark that is
my life; for all
of my days, back out
away from the shore
where

the waves are
high and the
wind is almost
stronger than the
strength of my
ship; and with Your
Pilot's hand
keep; the rudder
into the storm, so
that when at
last the ship of
my life has
found the other
shore; I will know,
really KNOW, I have
crossed where the
tides both came in
and went out.

We Want

We want back
what we have
thrown
away and
want it
shining
like it
did when it was
new — quite
like
children who
lick
away the
lollipop and then
long to see
it's
bright
red face
again — —

Every Child

Dear tiny
child, God's little
girl; so fresh from
His own
planning and
shaping AND
DE-
SIGNING... tiny nose and
tiny toes, petal ears and quick little dimpled
yawns; cheeks pressed in
place by the Gentle
Jesus who
said,
"Suffer these little ones to
come to Me"
Great glistening
tears and big, mean sudden
fears, Tiny wiggly body; (Just the
right size) see the
smile — — —
staying there for just
a little
while.

Sir Rederick — My Friend

He is not
gone; the
gentle
friend — though it
could
seem so; by the
absence
of the familiar
bark — and the
ever-wagging
tail — but it is
not
so, and on
snowy nights
and
sunny days or
rainy
afternoons I see
him still with
the old joy; bounding
across the
yard from favorite
tree to
favorite
tree — —

Middle School — First Week

See the fear there
In his
Eyes.... That
Laughter will
Follow him to the
Seat... (there in the
Third row)... It
Happens
Every year, come
September — the
Faces change but
Not the
Things they
Say or
Do — so
He blinks; sets his
Jaw and
Waits... For
The hurt
To
Happen.

The Great Gift

So many of
the special things
God
has given us
to love
are small.
Not needing to
loom before us
to touch
our hearts
The blossom of
a wildflower
tucked beneath an
evergreen tree by a
Mighty hand.
A brief greeting from
one
we love
A cotton kitten
reminding us

of the miracle
of birth;
Brightly colored
tiny bird
sharing
a song; a
butterfly
nervously seeking;
tiny, many-
legged creatures,
wondrous to behold;
and
most particularly
LITTLE PEOPLE
who hold
our hearts
in child-sized palms.

Silence

Red is gone, the
friendly — "please
hear
me" bark is
still, the bright
eyes, the
heart that
overflowed and
dauntless, returned
reproof with
love; is
quiet now — The joy
in snow and summer days; the love for
us all who
filled his
world; how
still — how
very still — —

And Welcome, Always Welcome, Always Yours

Come, walk with us,
down the street with the funny trees
See it there — fourth on the right
The old house
where the door is never locked
Always open to welcome
And love waits inside...

That worn old place right there
Where light smiles in the windows
A place where no one is a stranger
And friend means family too!...

See them; the great old trees
protecting memories stored in every rafter
You know, sometimes on still & snowy nights
You can hear long ago laughter
And feel salty tears.... sometimes

A mystery marching across the years
Mingling.... yesterdays; todays;
And the excitement of tomorrows
In the magic that is home.

Tomorrow

Little girl, sitting
at the
big desk, pre-
tending to be
grown... You need
not know for now how
much it will hurt to
come to that Reality that Robs; where
pretending
stops being your
shining
castle — —

This November —
Like Some Others —

Darkness was
slicing the
gray time between
dusk and dawn when the
first snow
flakes fell; and I
cried... remembering when
I believed we would
share the
first of
everything each
year; the first crocus
in the spring, and the
first robin
outside our
window, the
earliest night sounds
of summer, and the first of every
new beginning; but
the snow; each
first snowfall, soft
dusting magic
over everyday places
and people and
things, that first
snow we would
always share; like
children; or
so we really did believe.

Inside Out

You ask me what I
think of the
changes that have
come; and I
say that they are
fine and just
as they should be. You
forget, I think
that I have
a longer than
long
history of saying
what I should and
doing just the
same.

The Secret the Leaves Told Me

Hear them? In the
darkness — early morn-
ing, long before
dawn tears
open the
sky, leaves rushing
about on crispy
feet outside
my window, so great is
their hurry to be
here — or there —
before day light knows
their secret and
shares it
with the sun's
rays, and tells it
to the
day.

The Loss

pretty pictures, made by
Square, and Sweet and
Little hands, pictures of
flowers and
faces and
imaginary lands... offered
to grown-ups to
keep and treasure; a gift
whose journey most
often is the
short
distance between broken
crayons and the
trash

...cruel adults who know no shame.

Discovery

While traveling down
the loathsome
road to
discouragement, I came upon--
and not by
chance--a
soul-saving
detour of
the noblest
kind. While
changing my
route it
changed me
too--and my
life never will
be

the same. And
that destination
which would
have been
depression,
discouragement and
delay; I never
did reach, for that
marvelous detour
in my way, led to
the road
called thinking
of others, and
it leads straight
to the door
of unspeakable
JOY.

Home

A house should
be large enough
to hold a
dream and
small enough to
surround
life that is
real--and
rich--and
rewarding--and
reaching out to
draw in--and
enfold those
fellow pilgrims
who might find
inside its
walls the love of
God and love of
friend--a house
that lets the
sunshine spill into
its rooms and
flood its soul on
any day and when the purple
shadows
circle it--a house that
sends warm light into
the nighttime to
welcome that one, a stranger
for a time--a house
where Love is
locked in and
loneliness is
locked out and
God spreads His
hand of protection
over those who
come and
go--and come

My Son

He was such a
little boy with his
tousled hair and
his great troubled
eyes and his heart that
was heavy and
broken--his world had
crashed all around him and I
stood so helpless to put it
together again—but I
told him of the
lovely Jesus who
cares and loves and
feels--and how He
hears each small
child's prayer and
knows a tear drop when
we cry--and I
told him of the
gentle hands that mend
a million worlds each
day; and of the heart of
a Galilean that
breaks with a thundering
sound and I told him of a
friend who would never
break his heart and I
promised my small sized
man that the strong
Carpenter would walk with
him when I no
longer could.

Yellow Bird

I watched the
tear slide down
her pink cheek and
past the
freckle on her
nose and tremble
there just like
the quivering in
her frightened little
heart; and I
knew that I must be
the hands of
Christ to soothe; and
the eyes of Christ
to see into the
hurt in hers; and I
knew that I must be
the compassion of
Christ to know
empathy and under-
standing and I knew
that I must be the
very Love of
Christ to mend the
broken places in
her gentle and tender
little heart...
It is what He has
called us to do; and be;
and know.

Little Man

Such a tiny
boy, Lord, and
so much expected of
him, in a
world that
never slows
down
for small
people and small
talk; or
little boys with dreams of
someday
things,... oh, dear
God, will
You, hear his
voice in all the
noise of
a world gone
mad; and build for
him a
one day dream?

Celebration

I am so
grateful, today,
Lord,
for the eyes of my soul.
I see so
much more than
a dappled summer
sky--but all
of eternity.
In the delicate wings
of a butterfly--all of
creation, and when
a graceful bird wings
overhead, he takes
with him the very soul of
me, and in
the power of a sudden
summer storm, I

know all of
your might, and
in the velvet
petals of
a baby's mouth I
see all of
Your gentleness, and
in the gnarled
hands of the
old, all of Your
Love--and in
the warmth of those
I love, my soul
beholds Your face
and the windows
of my soul, I
know will
never dim

The Man in Denim

Minister Brown is
now and again a
little sad.. . He thinks of
the
church he wishes
he had. . . . humming along
the hallways; he cleans and
sings and al-
most hears the
choir's ring, The amens are
loud and
his preaching clear ...   Janitor
Brown believes the
answer to prayer
may even be
near

Significant

No one to
talk
to when the hour is
late; or the
heart is
heavy; no
one to listen to
the hurt
when darkness is
inside and
out; Not one of the
masses that
swarm all
day that cares (or
even knows)
that I'm dying in-
side, that
I ache for the
words I read there
in Webster's
red book,...cher-
ish, tenderness, and
even only God
knows the
saddest of all, im-
portant, de-
fined on page
156 as
"significant."

Remembrance

For just a little
while; on a
winter day I
held a
velvet and
summer butterfly in
my outstretched
hand; but I
knew his heart
had a
wanderlust and
I knew he would
not stay; and I
cried that
day for
what
might be; and for
what I prayed
would not; and I
kept the
wonder till
springtime came
and locked it in
my heart; but
the butterfly had a
winter soul and he
was gone one
warm and orange
afternoon and
I?

True Friendship

O Lord, dear
Lord; give me a
Love not
unlike Your own; a
love that can
encompass those that
are not
pretty and those
that are not
loveable--give me
words to transfer
faith to those
who cannot
believe in
themselves; and
trust to
those who walk in
fear. Let me
share strength
when weakness brings
defeat and give me
words that hold
wisdom when answers
are not there; Let it
be Your strong
heart and not my
own that responds
to needs that
overwhelm and when
someone lonely and lost
needs to find the
way; be in me and
let the path I lead
him to be Your own
straight way...

Gospel Given

I can see the imprints
of the scars in the
handprints of
Jesus Christ where
He touches
your life; and see the
dusty foot-
prints on the
paths of
your days; where He
walks beside
you; quietly and
sometimes when
you think that
He does not,
and in your
actions feel the
Galilean
who was but a
Carpenter and
a lonely
Nazarene.

Affirmation

A sister in
the faith...How
blessed
the very words; the thought the
truth, holy
calling from a
God of
Love...Words to
encourage, Love to
share, Prayers to
lift the
offered and the
offerer. A sister in
faith of the
faithful; sojourner sister
of the
Christ.

Good Bad Friday

During these three
hours on an
ordinary seeming
day--the
skies grow
overcast and
morose in
remembrance of Your
agonizing on
the hill of
retribution and the
air holds a
scent of mystery as
earth and
You recall the
draining blood and
the price of
life--and yet with
this
clearly providential
phenomenon--the
horns blow and the busses smoke and
the buying and
selling of the frills
and
pastels that are
Easter goes on
unaware even
nature weeps to
remember--

Elation

This early morning
when a rain-
refreshed world
quivers and
sings with the
gift of
Life; I feel
deeply humbled, dear
Jesus; awed by the
sacred and
silver
silences that are
ours -- those
spun-glass
moments when we
say nothing and
our hearts speak... when
You stoop down to
speak to us; and we
are privileged to
hear each other;
and You!

Strength

When the pounding
waves rush across
my soul, and meet the
black clouds up
above, and the
rushing wind
around sends fear
across my
heart, when
answers to
ugly giants
cannot be
found, in the
center of
this, Great
God, I thank you
for the quiet
peace that
comes in a
wonderfully
gentle -smile; and
the softness of
a rich voice, and
the trust that
is Your gift
for
the laughter that
helps me to
forget and the
Holy Spirit to
remind me that
my life; for all of
it's lasting   is. . .
in Your strong
Hands. . .

Petition

Dear God
in the early morning light
I study
those dishes
Left last night
piled in the sink.
The day was not
put together well . . .
Drawn properly to conclusion . . .
Or they would not be there
And I would have waken today
More serene . . . more victorious . . .
God of Power, let me close this day
In a better way, at my sink . . .
and in my heart.

And So?

At that altar where
Calvary covered
the corners of
my life; and I gave
my promise and
my possessions to
Jesus Christ; I
believed I could lay
down the dreams
and the doubts and
desires that
were mine; and in
His power I
have; but
today with
the fragments of
a broken
heart shattered
before me; and
inside me; I
fight the
person I am
who wants that
beautiful and
shiny thing that
is just outside
the reach of
the will of
God . . .

Walking and Running

It was just ordinary
people Jesus called
to walk with
Him.. .unusual only
because they
laid down their
nets. And so
it is in
our world to-
day. Every-day
ones like you and
I; who work and
play; and weep and
pray. Weary ones who
have given up; and
seekers after a
star--men and
women of every
trade to follow a gentle
Carpenter; and
children to walk
in the footsteps of
a man as old as
God; and not
quite thirty-two.
Just ordinary
city-dwellers and
humble country-
folks that He
still calls
to follow Him to
the City Eternal to
be lifted to the
throne of
God.

Bright Morning

We have come in
confession Lord,
on this spring-time
day. Admitting to
each other; and
to You--our
Father confessor; and
above all
forgiver; we have
laid before Your
Altar-heart our
narrowness; our
angers; our
pettiness; even
our
hatreds. There
are empty and
dark places,
Lord, where all
of these have
been in the
hall-ways of
our
hearts. . .Fill
those echoing
spaces, dear
Jesus, with Your
own wide horizons
where there was
narrowness; Your
gentleness where
angels have been, and
the bigness of
Your vision where
pettiness had taken up
abode; and pour the
clear and sparkling
waters of Your love
into the cavern where
hatred lurked--
and having done
all of this,
remind our
rebel hearts, that
we are Your
own.

Fellow Traveler

Sometimes I need to
stand on the green
moss carpet outside the
empty tomb; to know
the return of the
dear Christ
who has seemed far
off and unfelt...
sometimes I need to
walk up the steep
way to a
darkened Calvary to
know the flood
of forgiveness
and sometimes I
kneel alone in the
quiet of my own
Gethsemane to know
the fountain of
sorrow--and on
starry snowy
nights I can hear the
lowing

cattle as I
approach the tiny
stable to find wonder
once again; and
when I need to
know the
presence of His
Power I stand
on Galilee's
shore to
watch a pure
white dove
descend to rest on
His strong
shoulder; and when
everything over-
whelms me I
walk dusty roads with
Him to learn once
again; to love
people as He
did....

Never-Ending

I celebrate little
Christmases. . . early ones, not
early at
all; for Christmas is
forever and all
year and every today, turning
corners of the old
house into
Christmas-quiet, finding
shining in the
stillness and wonder walking
through the memories and
mystery in the
truth of a
tumble-
down
stable. . .

The Christ

There was the
shadow of a
cross
on that manger so
long ago--and
in the dim
light that
flickered;
Mary saw it
and
brushed away a
tear--gentle
lady with the
broken heart, and
Joseph--solid,
strong, felt the
sharp tug of
pain within
his chest
because the
journey had not
ended here in
sweet smelling
hay; and these
two chosen both
knew it had
only begun

Boxes & Bundles

We have categorized
Your world, Lord, the
people of Your
creation; Forgive us
for the harm we
do in our
decision who will
be a hood; or
a greaser, or who
has charisma and
who does not; we
think we can
determine who
serves no
purpose and who
strives for
worthy goals; and
who it is with
qualifications to
make it; and who
might as well
quit; we glue
sticky labels onto
people we have
never met because of
what they wear or
say or do not
do--and in our
mockery of wisdom
we really do not
have we forgot that
beneath those red and
blue labels are hearts and
souls and feelings; and
hurts just like
our own.

2002

Beauty scattered in
Shadows of
New
Budding leaves
Dancing on
An afternoon
Window
Pane . . lemon-
Lime green willow
Sprouts, waving
Branches rejoicing in
Promise
Fulfilled, the song
Of each small
Bird . . . new
Lives, cold, featherless,
Fragile, new blades of
Grass mark the carpet
To
Come, afternoon sun
Painting color on
Silk and shiny
New
Leaves . . . .

The people I
Have known . . . a
Parade of past re-
membrances on
Review . . . the grocer; there
On the corner, the boy at the
gas
Station – who smiled on
Sunday morning and
Every
Other morning too . . Across
The street and down the
Block . . . GONE: Where? I do
Not know . . . but for a
Time along this
Journeys way . . . bright
And blessed markings on
The path of the
Heart as the wending
Of the
Way . . . .

A New Year

A New Year? With
All of its
Fresh starts,
Its resolutions,
profound
Plans; the
Wiping and the washing
Away of what has
Gone before.
The tiny, trembling
Fears of what it
Will hold; even
The awesomeness of
Its promise. It
Looms large and unknown ---
Keep reminding me dear Jesus,
That you are
The Alpha and
The Omega and
That it is
Only new to me.

Death

death, seek to
destroy if
you
will, friend
or family, or
worse still
a pet, the friend
of friends to
me; but you
cannot, rob my
heart, my
soul, my memory, my
mind - and
there (and
here) the
love lives on and you, cannot,
no you
cannot nor ever shall
erase what
has been and
always will
be -

I Believe

For the
Small
Miracles of
Answered
Prayer, those
Quiet
Affirmations
That You
Hear the
Whispered
Pleas that
Slip from
Trembling lips
And
Cry from
Aching
Hearts . . . For
The
Larger
Miracles that
Come with
July fourth
Fanfare and
Shout Your might
To those
Who
Can't
Believe and
For your
Heart of Love
That decides which
Size
Miracle I
Need . . Thank
You Lord!

I Would Be a Bridge

I would be a
Bridge for
You to
Step across – a
Span to under-
Standing the person
That you
Are – and I would
Cover the
Troubled waters that
Sometimes
Overwhelm and then
Be your stepping
Place to the
Grassy other
Side - I would be
there for you to
tread across when you
need to
walk away; And
be ready to fill the
chasm of your
discontent – I would
be strong for you
to walk upon and
encourage you as
you journey
across – and be
always quietly
waiting when you
need to step
back again --

If I Hurt

If I hurt
and need your help –
do not offer
me more
platitudes and
if I hurt
do not
cover my
gaping wounds
with star and
stripe
cliché's; or
toss out neat
round life lines
of scripture -
taken out of their
context; and mine - - that you may slap my fingers (or my
spirit); to tell me what
you think I
should do – instead,
love me enough to see if
I am
able - - if I hurt!

Hurried Hours

If I were to
stop the
hurried hours of
this dreadful
day; and had the
power to
hold the hours
suspended for a
while and
we; you and I
could be
alone with no
sound to
break the silence or
the spell;   still
with all of
that I
would not be
able to tell you the
things I
really am; and I
guess I
really know it
doesn't matter any-
way;

June 1984

Why oh why
Lord have
You asked more
Than I
Can give and your
Taking torn
The gaping
Hole in my
Heart that never
Will mend? - The
Place where the memories
pour out – tripping
And
Rumbling and
Crashing across my
Mind –
Drowning in
The valley of
My tears and
Floating up to
Drift across
These waves of
Grief that rise and
Fall - turning hours to days –
And days
To endless
Aching – Memories
Of first steps,
And first days of
School and
First hurts and
Growing up steps
And
Plans – oh! Those
Plans for tomorrows –
And the new beginnings;

And dreams
Waiting on teen –
Age calendars to
Come true – and
Special Christmas's
And Birthday
Candles – put out by tear drops
now –
Here in my
Quiet room – the
Feeling proud –
Sometimes frustrated...

Solitude

When I search
The life of another
For the imprint of
God,
And do not find it there,
And I look into the face
Of one I have admired,
But the reflection
Of Christ is gone;
And I cannot feel Him
Closer in the rows of books
On narrow shelves; and
Chapel walls only echo
Emptiness and it seems
He is not there . . . I find
A place of quiet, where
People have not been . . .
Where trees and sky are
Walls and ceiling to my
Cathedral, and birds the
Organ play . . .here I always
Find Him and here He
Always speaks; for He, too,
Sometimes seeks the
Silences of His world . . .
And my soul.

All Are Family

Thanksgiving once again
      and
It's a small World afterall
don't you see
And all of us are family-

It's a small afterall
Different colors, different
noses, different jobs and
different
clothes –
Different goals and
different skills –
financiers and some
with bills
Some of us are BIG and
Some of us small – Athletes or
sitters upon our
sit –upons –
Loud or quiet – Chubby or
Thin – Still if you're one of
this family you're IN!!!

Because it's a small world
afterall; Some of us
drink – some of us don't –
Some of us cuss (really?)
others won't –
Smoke or Spit or chew –
different me – different you –
Some of us may want a lot –
(coming from the land of have
not)
others don't care what they've
got –

One thing in common and
don't let's forget –
We're all still
here - - at least yet!

Oldest to youngest, family by
family and face by
face – We're all God's children
Yesireeee
And through it all
Still family

Fine dining is great for some
other's wait till the food
stamps come
just so we all respect each
other
Always a sister – Always a
brother –

Cause it's a small world afterall
and nobody Knows about
tomorrow –
Troubles come along and so
does
                  sorrow –
If my world's up and yours is
down
It's sure as heck to turn around
–

Nobody's perfect – at least not
me

But I'm proud to be part of
your
                    family –

You're the greatest bunch of
turkeys don't you see –
if you look around and see
                    someone strange
And wonder if they'll ever
                    change
The answer to the above –
is a 4 – letter word called Love

Thanks for being right by my
                    side
On a summer night when I
                    almost died –
"Croaked" is what I'm want to
                    say –
But thank you muchly anyhow

Cause it's a small world afterall
And all are family –
Each & every one

That Cross

Jesus chose twelve
Rough, and rugged, and
Rowdy men; Unschooled, and
Unskilled and slightly
Uncouth; Then when
He wanted to
Tame them and
Train them – and sophisticate their
Senses - - He chose
His own blood and
Sweat hewn tool; <u>the</u>
One handed
Down from his own
Father and
Carved of Love ....for
He Knew and they
Knew - that cross on
Golgotha's hill
Would not Save One Soul
Not Strong <u>or willing</u> -
<u>Enough</u>-to be
Broken.

The First Step

Beginnings need
Not
Come in Years,
Millenniums or
Defined
Historical periods, the
Victorian, the
Industrial,
The Roaring 20's or
The skeptical sixties – not in
The New Moon or
The four
Season's turning
In time; Not in
Remorse or
Resolution, or
Promises to
Change – A
Be-
Ginning of the
Most
Profound
Kind leaps out
Each
Time a
Sinner says
Yes to
Jesus Christ!

Easter Morning

To touch
And feel and know
Those sacred
Things
Unseen that come
From
He who is Spirit
And Son of
God alone...things
Eternal, holy, mysterious un –
Believable
Yet real; a voice
To be heard in
The
Secret chambers of
A soul, audible
Only in a
Heart - - Easter Morning -   a
Coming of the
Christ!!!

Yesterday, Tomorrow and Today!

There may be
Other days and other
Nights; time
For things to
Do and calendars
Marked with
Important
Nothings in
Every square with
Red and blue
To separate
Your things
Essential from
Mine; but there will
Not be another
Repeat of
This right now
Moment when

I have needed you
And needed
To feel
Safe; to
Share the ache
Inside of me and so
The important things will be
x'd off
And the calendar
Will be filled with
Perfect
Priorities and I; I
Will grow
Weary of the
Waiting and know why
I have stopped
Believing

Your Room

Inside your
room? For-
bidden
place-not
even a
crack open
wide
enough to see in-
side or allow
a
glimpse of
who is
there—while
you step outside to
say
what seems
right and do
your
daily things while
still
keeping who
your are in
that
secret place a
mystery that
separates our hearts by
more than just a
door

End or Beginning - KiKi

End or
Beginning – the
Senior
Year? The
Smile at the future – the tear
For the
Past -? A
Start - - a
Finish – to each
His own – for
The one
Standing by –
Memories roll
like a slow
moving film
the gone by so
familiar – what is
aged so
nearly frightening
even
in the light of faith -

Shhhhh!

There is a
Deeper side of
Life
Than the hellos
And
Goodbye's for every –
Day – a sanctuary
Kind
Of place when
Feelings flow on a
River of
Teardrops
And joy when
It
Comes is not in
Laughter
But quiet breaths
Of
thanksgiving

Time

In the
Autumn of my
Life
Saying thanks and
Praise
Seem to be a single rising
Scent of the
Incense
Of joy – a
Blending of the
Ears (so many)
When the
Two cannot
Be separated!

October

I read of the
World
Around me each
Morning - -
And I gaze
Around
At my own – quite
Unkempt and
Needing
"doing" –
The long
Awaiting organizing - -
But – I
Felt the
Remembrance of
Years – and
I pause; extend
My heart to thank
You Lord
For this dear
World!
Mine!
Always Mine!

Tanner

He is just
A little boy
Lord – (though
Taller than
Last year's
First day of
Learning) on
The way to
Man – - not
Knowing that these
Times of
Lessons and
Friends, snow time
And spring,
Grades and guessing,
Triumphs (though
Small) and
Tears, (though large)
Will one day mark
Growing up – but
For today,
Please remember
Lord, that he is
Just a little
Boy!

The Answer?

God?
Therapy?
Healing is a
Sometimes thing – or
Sometimes
Not at
All – but when it
Does its
Work of powers
Lives are
Changing
The
Light is
Brighter and
Can you
Hear
The Song?
Can you?

The Crickets Question

Would I go
Back if I could to the
Night we
First
Met – and the
Spark's – (unseen)
That were
in the
Air – Or on the
Notes of
Music – why of
Course I
Would – and
Would I
Be able to
Remember each
First
Word – (Smile)
(hug) – thought – (though
Forbidden it
Be) – how long ago was
Yesterday after
All! - ??

I Believe

So they say
That
Growing older has
A name
(or many) like
Elderly senior (God
Forbid that one) or
Aged or the softly
Spoken, "she's
Pretty old you
Know" – covering slow
And
Senile in one phrase – or
Long lived even if
Those years were en –
dured and not really, really
loved – wrong, wrong
all of
them – An Awakening is a glorious name for
Now!

The Child

If the
Child
Who
Once
Breathed
Life into
Imagination
Were no
Longer me,
What a rickety
Broken
Thing old
Age would
Be – oh but
She
Still
Sees the
Fairies
Dancing and
Disguised
As rain –
Drops –
And
Knows
The
Gasshopper
Does
Wave a
Greeting
To
The child
Lying in
The grass

Intrepid Ink

About Intrepid Ink, LLC

Intrepid Ink, LLC provides full publishing services to authors of fiction and non-fiction books, eBooks and websites. From editing to formatting, from publishing to marketing, Intrepid Ink gets your creative works into the hands of the people who want to read them. Find out more at www.IntrepidInk.com.

www.ingramcontent.com/pod-product-compliance
Lightning Source LLC
Chambersburg PA
CBHW072157090426
42740CB00012B/2298